World Cup
Soccer Stars

D0517816

TRIUMPH
BOOKS

Triumph Books
542 South Dearborn Street
Suite 750
Chicago, IL 60605
Phone: (312) 939-3330
Fax: (312) 663-3557
www.triumphbooks.com

Printed in the United States of America
ISBN: 978-1-60078-367-8

Content developed & packaged by Mojo Media, Inc.
Editor: Joe Funk
Creative Director: Jason Hinman

Photos courtesy AP Images unless otherwise indicated

Contents

The World Cup 2010 mascot waves during a friendly match in South Africa.

Introduction to the
2010 World Cup

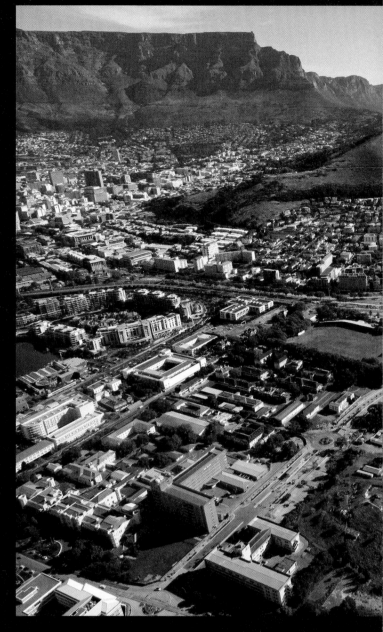

An African country will host soccer's global championship for the first time when the FIFA World Cup 2010 is played in South Africa. This is an amazing opportunity for South Africa, which from 1961 to 1991 was not even allowed to play international soccer because the country's government policy of Apartheid—a legal system that mandated racial segregation. When the country peacefully eliminated the unfair system, their soccer team was welcomed back into international play, and in 2004 they were further rewarded with the 2010 World Cup.

After a two-year-long qualifying tournament, 32 teams from six regions earned the right to play in the finals. As host, South Africa earned an automatic bid; five other African nations qualify. The other regions, and the number of qualifiers from each, are: Europe, 13; South America, 4; Asia, 4; and CONCACAF (North America, Central America, Caribbean), 3. The two final spots are decided by an Oceania/Asia playoff and a South America/CONCACAF playoff.

The favorites going into South Africa should be the world's two top-ranked teams, Brazil and Spain. In addition, the Netherlands, Germany, Italy, and England all played well throughout the qualification rounds and will enter the tournament with high hopes. The U.S. team narrowly defeated their main rivals, Mexico, to win the CONCACAF region and will go to the 2010 World Cup hoping to match or better their previous best finishes—third place in 1934 and the quarterfinals in 2002.

In the six years leading up to the finals, South Africa has worked furiously to prepare for the tournament. The biggest challenge was readying world-class 10 stadiums in nine different cities for playing the 64 games that make up the tournament. Five of the stadiums are brand-new. The other five venues were preexisting but expanded and renovated. The South African stadiums include some of the most unique designs that the world has ever seen, sporting arenas fitting for such an important and memorable event.

As with all World Cups, the big draw for fans will be watching the planet's top players go head to head with soccer's biggest prize on the line. The pages that follow introduce several of the stars who are expected to shine brightest in South Africa.

③

South Africa has done an incredible job of building stadiums and preparing to host the World Cup.

1. Green Point Stadium will host a number of games in Cape Town. Thousands of people are expected to visit the Western Cape Province during the 2010 World Cup.

2. A huge soccer ball sits atop Lukasrand Telkom Tower in Pretoria. The ball is 80 feet across and eight stories high and was built explicitly for FIFA's 2010 World Cup.

3. Perhaps the most coveted team trophy on the entire planet, the competition for the World Cup is truly a global passion.

4. A child kicks a soccer ball in the shadows of Royal Bafokeng Stadium near Rustenburg. The stadium, owned by the Bafokeng tribe, will be among 10 across South Africa hosting World Cup matches.

1. An aerial view of Johannesburg and Hillbrow in late 2009. Johannesburg is one of the host cities for the 2010 World Cup.

2. The fans in soccer-crazy South Africa are excited to host the World Cup—and to showcase their extraordinary country to the rest of the world.

3. A worker on the roof of the Soccer City Stadium, site of the 2010 World Cup final, in October 2009 as the stadium nears completion.

4. An aerial view of the Mbombela Stadium under construction in Nelspruit in September 2009.

5. Peter Mokaba Stadium in Polokwane nears completion in September 2009.

Landon Donovan

UNITED STATES OF AMERICA

Hometown: Ontario, California

"Anything with the ball is the best thing you can do, everything else will come to you later, just be with the ball as much as possible."

– Landon's advice to young players

The biggest star of United States soccer in this generation, Landon Donovan has had a career full of ups and downs. From his pedigree with the national team development program to disaster in Europe, to a rebirth back home, the 27-year-old has done it all in the last decade.

Unlike most players in the United States, Donovan never played college soccer. Going pro at age 18 instead, he figured heavily in the future plans of German squad Bayer Leverkusen. To further season Donovan, they returned him on load to the San Jose Earthquakes of the MLS to get game experience.

Donovan became a star in San Jose, quickly proving himself to be a gifted goal-scorer. He starred for the U.S. team at the 2000 Olympics in Australia and became a full member of the national squad later that year.

Landon figured heavily in the U.S. run in the 2002 World Cup, finding the back of the net twice. With his career on the rise, Bayer decided to recall him from loan in 2005. The Bundesliga, however, was not kind to Donovan and he made just seven appearances for the team before being sold to MLS.

He found himself allocated to the L.A. Galaxy, and immediately established himself as a leader on the squad. Now playing with David Beckham on that club and with another World Cup under his belt, fans should be excited to see what Donovan does next. Throughout qualifying, he was the American team's top playmaker—he has the skills to carry the team deep into the tournament.

Fast Stat:

1

Donovan is the Number One goal-scorer and assist man in United States national team history.

Ht: 5' 8" • **Wt:** 175 • **DOB:** 3/4/1982

Position: Midfield/Striker

2009–2010 Salary: $900,000

International goals/International caps:
42 goals/120 caps

Personal homepage:
www.landondonovan.com

Did you know?: The entire time Donovan played for the San Jose Earthquakes, he was on loan from his German club

As a kid: Landon played with several U.S. teammates with the national team development program in Bradenton, Florida

Favorite food: Crab meat

Hobbies: Landon enjoys outdoor activities and travel.

Favorite music: Landon will listen to anything, especially when it comes to getting pumped up for a game.

Tim Howard

UNITED STATES OF AMERICA

Hometown: North Brunswick, New Jersey

One of the finest goalkeepers in the world, Tim Howard has been wowing spectators in the English Premier League since his high-pressure stint at Manchester United proved that the United States' top 'keeper belonged on the world-class stage.

Despite becoming a household name for Man U fans, Howard soon became a forgotten man. The arrival of Edwin van der Sar and Tomasz Kuszczak pushed Howard down the team's goalkeeping pecking order—just another test for Howard in a career full of challenges. He eventually caught on with Everton where he has rewritten the record books with four seasons of dominant play in front of the net.

The New Jersey native began playing midfielder and keeper in high school and started his professional career with the North Jersey Imperials at the young age of 17. He joined the MLS New York–New Jersey Metrostars in 1998.

Eventually replacing U.S. soccer legend Tony Meola as the Metrostars goalkeeper, Howard stayed with the team for six seasons and established himself as one of Major League Soccer's most talented—and most popular—players. And with the international retirement of Kasey Kellar, Howard stepped into goal for the U.S. and quickly became of the leaders of the national team.

Howard is a devout Christian and has fought a well-publicized battle with Tourette syndrome, a condition that leads him to have involuntary tics and impulses. He is involved in creating awareness for the disorder and was named to the board of directors of the Tourette Syndrome Association of New Jersey in November 2001. His charitable efforts have seen him earn the New York Life Humanitarian of the Year award.

Fast Stat:

4

Clean sheets by Tim to start the 2009–2010 season

Ht: 6' 3" • **Wt:** 210 • **DOB:** 3/6/1979

Position: Goalkeeper

2009–2010 Salary: undisclosed

International goals/International caps: 0 goals/48 caps

Personal homepage: www.timhowardstory.com

Did you know?: Howard averaged 15 points per game on the basketball court in high school.

As a kid: Time had to overcome the difficulties brought on by Tourette syndrome to excel as an athlete.

Fun tidbit: Howard played in his first professional game a month before he graduated high school

Hobbies: Sleeping, charity work, and inspiring others with Tourette syndrome

Favorite music: Faith-based music and anything to get pumped up before a game

"Tim is now on the same level as Pepe Reina and Petr Cech. They are considered to be the two best in England. I would not swap either for my man." —David Moyes

Cuauhtemoc Blanco

MEXICO

Hometown: Mexico City

Cuahutemoc Blanco is regarded as one of Mexico's best attacking midfielders and one of the Primera Division's most prolific scorers, with 151 goals. He has amassed 107 caps and scored 37 goals for his country, but he is best known in the United States for his highlight-reel goals with the Chicago Fire. One of the signature stars of MLS, Blanco is greeted by legions of fans wherever the Fire play.

Blanco has played for the Mexican national team in two World Cups, 1998 and 2002, scoring in each one of them. He was a member of the Mexican national team that won the Confederations Cup in 1999 where he was the tournament's leading scorer with six goals, including one in the final. He won the Golden Boot for his performance, earning the man of the tournament award as well.

After a lull in his national team form, Blanco is back in the top graces of Mexican coaches, mostly due to his experience and current play with the Chicago Fire. On September 13, 2008, the veteran playmaker earned his 100th cap for his country in its 2–1 World Cup qualifier victory over Canada at home, coming on with only 15 seconds left in regulation. On October 10, 2009, Blanco scored the second goal in a 4–1 victory over El Salvador to help Mexico clinch a spot in the 2010 World Cup.

"He just floats around the field."

—Seattle Sounders FC coach Sigi Schmid

Fast Stat:

16

Goals Blanco has scored in his 61 career MLS games

Ht: 5' 10" • **Wt:** 180 • **DOB:** 1/17/1973

Position: Attacking midfielder

2009–2010 Salary: $2.6 million

International goals/International caps: 107/37

Personal homepage: none

Did you know?: Blanco's favorite American food is McDonalds' Big Macs.

As a kid: Blanco developed his signature "Blanco Trick" while playing with older kids. He needed a move to get around the faster, bigger players and developed the trick as a way to avoid tackles.

Favorite food: Pancita

Hobbies: Dancing, watching boxing

Favorite music: Anything he can dance to

Giovani dos Santos

MEXICO

Hometown: Monterrey

Only 20 years old, Giovani dos Santos has already amassed an impressive trophy case of awards and accolades in his short career. His international reputation is also growing steadily thanks to his knack for playing best in big games.

The Mexican international competes in the English Premiership for Tottenham Hotspur, playing in an attacking midfield spot for Spurs after spending last season on loan at Ipswich Town. He has not quite found his scoring touch at the top level in England, but he has been at his best when wearing his homeland's colors.

He scored his first two goals for Mexico on June 24, 2009, in a friendly match against Venezuela, a game in which he was also named man of the match. He scored his third goal for Mexico on July 19 in the 2009 CONCACAF Gold Cup quarterfinal game against Haiti, chipping in with two assists in a 4–0 Mexican win.

In July 2009, he helped Mexico end a 10-year winless drought against the United States on American soil with a 5–0 victory at Giants Stadium in New York, putting the finishing touches on the team's Gold Cup championship. He also received the MVP award for the best player in the tournament. In September 2009, dos Santos contributed to all three goals in a 3–0 win over Costa Rica in World Cup qualification. He's a young player with a bright future at the club level, but in the international game he's already a player to be reckoned with.

Fast Stat:

0

Goals given up by Mexico in the five games dos Santos has scored in

Ht: 5' 8" • **Wt:** 175 • **DOB:** 5/11/89

Position: Attacking midfielder

2009–2010 Salary: $6.5 million

International goals/International caps: 5 goals/22 caps

Personal homepage: www.giodosantos.com

Did you know?: Giovani's brothers both play professional soccer. One plays in Mexico, the other in Spain for Barcelona.

As a kid: In addition to playing for club teams in Mexico, Giovani's dad, Gerardo dos Santos, played for the Brazilian national team.

Favorite foods: Anything healthy

Hobbies: Dancing and sleeping

Favorite music: Anything with a good beat to dance to

"Playing in England has been a great experience. I love the fans."
—dos Santos on his time with Tottenham

Wayne Rooney

England

Hometown: Liverpool

Born and raised an Everton fan, young Wayne Rooney has been in the spotlight from a very young age. With a skill and passion for the game noticed by many, it seemed only fitting that Rooney's first professional club was the one that he grew up following.

As a teen, Rooney found much success with the Everton youth squad that reached the Youth Cup final in 2002, earning him quick promotion to the first team. Against Arsenal later that year, Rooney became the youngest goal scorer in the Premier League, a goal that prompted the television commentator to exclaim, "Remember the name: Wayne Rooney!" Two seasons with Everton's first team and increasing pressure from local fans caused the talented young Englishman to seek out a transfer, and Manchester United was quick to snap him up.

Despite the increased media blitz surrounding him, Rooney has continued to excel at both the club and international levels. Rooney became a mainstay for the English squad soon after his transfer to Manchester United, a feat no doubt helped by his impressive performances in the Euro 2004 tournament. Rooney went on to make the World Cup squad in 2006, but had a disappointing tournament that ended with an unfortunate red card. He has bounced back and will surely feature on England's 2010 World Cup team, showing he's in top form by leading the team in scoring, with nine goals, during the qualifying rounds.

Fast Stat:

3

Goals scored by Wayne in his first Manchester United match

Ht: 5' 10" • **Wt:** 170 • **DOB:** 10/24/85

Position: Midfield/Striker

2009–2010 Salary: $9.8 million

International goals/International caps: 25 goals/55 caps

Personal homepage: www.waynerooney.com

Did you know?: When Wayne was called up for his first international game, he thought it was for the U-21 team.

As a kid: Wayne is the oldest of three children, and enjoyed spending time with his siblings.

Favorite food: Spaghetti bolognese

Hobbies: Wayne enjoys playing video games, especially FIFA Soccer

Favorite music: Eminem, 50 Cent

> *"We have got the best young player this country has seen for the past thirty years."*
>
> —Manchester United Manager Sir Alex Ferguson

Wayne Rooney is one of the brightest young stars in the game today. He plays for the world's biggest soccer club and is already an internationally known star. Although he hasn't yet had major success in the World Cup finals, fans are cautioned to remember the name: Wayne Rooney.

Steven Gerrard

ENGLAND

Hometown: Whiston

An inspiring and commanding player, Steven Gerrard may mean more to his team and its fans than any other player in the world. Born and raised near Liverpool, Gerrard has never played for any other squad and is the heart and soul of the current team. Having stated that he has no intentions of ever leaving the club, Gerrard provides a stability in the midfield that no other team can hope to replicate. Even more impressive, he remains among the top midfielders in the world and competes at an impressive level on the international stage.

Discovered as a school boy at just 8 years old, Gerrard has been a part of the fabric of Liverpool for nearly his entire life. Despite an injury-plagued junior career with the club, he made his first team debut at just 18 years old in 1998. By the next season, he had quickly established himself as a regular on a club destined for greatness in the coming decade.

Awards and accolades continued to follow for Gerrard, and in 2002 he was named to England's World Cup team. Unfortunately, Steven was suffering from injuries relating to a late growth spurt and was unable to compete. He appeared for England in the tournament in 2006, leading the team in scoring with his two goals.

Gerrard remained a key player for the national team as they easily moved through World Cup qualifying, scoring three goals in the process. He also served as the team's vice captain as they stormed towards the tournament in South Africa.

"I'm a fan myself and I'm frustrated just as much as them when we get beat."

—Steven Gerrard on what Liverpool's success means to him

Fast Stat:

23

Goals Gerrard scored from his midfield position in 2005–2006

Ht: 6' 1" • **Wt:** 180 • **DOB:** 5/30/80

Position: Midfield

2009–2010 Salary: $12.75 million

International goals/International caps: 16 goals/76 caps

Personal homepage: www.liverpoolfc.tv/team/squad/gerrard/

Did you know?: Steven published an autobiography in 2006.

As a kid: Steven suffered from drastic growth spurts, stopping him from playing for long stretches at a time.

Favorite foods: Chicken, rice, and Caribbean food.

Hobbies: Steven enjoys collecting cars and driving them. He also enjoys golfing and playing pool.

Favorite music: Dance

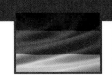

Miroslav Klose

GERMANY

Hometown: Opole, Poland

One of the most deadly strikers in the world, Bayern Munich forward Miroslav Klose is the face of Germany's Bundesliga and one of the signature names on the German national team. For the Polish-born Klose, however, it was a tough hurdle to accept all the attention from a country that he adopted.

For a man that considers himself a European citizen and a native of the world, he's been stunning when he's put on national colors. His consistency as a goal-scorer in his first Bundesliga season at Kaiserslautern earned him attention. In January 2001, then–national coach Jerzy Engel of Poland traveled to Germany to persuade Klose to choose to play for his team.

It was too late, as Klose had already chosen to utilize his German passport to play for the country. He soon was capped and made his debut for Germany against Albania on March 24, 2001. Klose came on as a substitute and headed in the winning 2–1 goal two minutes from time, an impressive debut.

Klose came to international prominence at the 2002 World Cup. He scored five goals, the second best total of the tournament. He scored five more goals at the 2006 World Cup—the last a dramatic equalizer in the quarterfinals against Argentina that made him the tournament's highest-scoring player. Klose was also Germany's top scorer leading up to the 2010 tournament, netting seven goals during the qualifying rounds.

1

Players that have scored five goals in two World Cups; Klose is the only one

Ht: 5' 11" • **Wt:** 165 • **DOB:** 6/9/78

Position: Striker

2009–2010 Salary: $8 million

International goals/International caps: 48 goals/93 caps

Personal komepage: www.miroslav-klose.de

Did you know?: Klose was the first player representing unified Germany to lead the World Cup in scoring.

As a kid: The Klose family spoke Polish at home and Miroslav learned German in kindergarten.

Fun tidbit: Klose's signature goal celebration is the front flip: he's been known to do multiple flips for particularly stunning goals.

Hobbies: Traveling and exploring new parts of the world

Favorite music: European pop

"It was a close decision to play for Germany, and not an easy one. I do not regret my choice, though."

Lukas Podolski

GERMANY

Hometown: Gilwice, Poland

Lukas Podolski has had an interesting rise in the soccer world. A Polish-born but distinctly German striker, Podolski made a name for himself thanks to a stirring performance in the 2006 World Cup, oddly enough while his club team sat mired in the second division. In fact, Podolski was the first German in decades to become a regular on the national team while playing in the second division.

Although Podolski had once rescued his Cologne team from the doldrums up to the Bundesliga, he was not around to do it a second time. His performance in Germany's ultimate third place finish was enough to secure him a transfer, and a big payday, with Bayern Munich, a dominating force in German soccer.

In 2008, Podolski became just the third German to score four goals in one international game. He has really shined brightest on an international stage, piling up the goals and leading Germany's 2010 World Cup qualifying group in scoring. Saving some of his best performances for Germany's toughest matches, Lukas Podolski is one of the best big-game strikers in the international game.

Fast Stat:

2

Podolski is one of two Polish-born players on the German national team

Ht: 5' 11" • **Wt:** 170 • **DOB:** 6/4/85

Position: Striker

2009–2010 Salary: $14.4 million

International goals/International caps: 35 goals/68 caps

Personal homepage: www.lukas-podolski.com

Did you know?: Lukas was born in Poland but his family moved to Germany when he was still a toddler

Fun tidbit: Lukas has appeared on the cover of the FIFA Soccer video game franchise in Germany

Hobbies: Basketball and music

Favorite music: Lukas will listen to anything, but enjoys dance

Luca Toni
ITALY
Hometown: Pavullo nel Frignano

We know his qualitiy and we need him."
—Bayern Munich President Karl-Heinz Rummenigge

When you start talking about Luca Toni, it all begins with one word: goals. It's simply what he does, better than nearly anyone else on the planet. His stats are impeccable, and when he is healthy, there may not be a more deadly striker playing the game.

As a player, Toni is an impressive specimen. Big and physical, he's adept at creating his own space in the box as well as leaping onto the ends of crosses to nod the ball past the keeper with authority. Luca also has a great ability to hold the ball up with his back to goal and allow for the rest of the team to join him in the attack, sending out some sweet passes in the process.

He scored his first international goal in a World Cup Qualifying match against Norway in September 2004, earning his first caps thanks to his stirring performance in bringing Palermo up to Serie A.

Toni was selected to Italy's 2006 World Cup squad and scored twice in the quarterfinals against Ukraine, his only goals of the tournament. He was called up to the Italian squad for Euro 2008, but was held scoreless.

Despite the Euro 2008 disappointment, Toni was selected by coach Marcello Lippi for Italy's 2010 World Cup team, showing that the nation still has faith in him. What's most impressive is that Toni is considered a late-bloomer in soccer. As late as age 26 he was playing second-division football, but his 30s have provided a breakout for the big Italian.

Fast Stat:

14

Goals in the Bundesliga for Toni in 2008–09, scored over just 25 games due to injury

Ht: 6' 5" • **Wt:** 210 • **DOB:** 5/26/77

Position: Striker

2009–2010 Salary: $7.4 million

International goals/International caps: 16 goals/47 caps

Personal homepage: www.lucatoni.com

Did you know?: Luca Toni won the European Golden Shoe in 2006 for scoring more club goals than any other player on the continent.

As a kid: Before he decided to stick to soccer, Luca Toni was a strong basketball player in his age group thanks to an early growth spurt.

Fun tidbit: Toni's personal motto is "Never give up!"

Hobbies: Fashion and acting

Favorite music: Anything joyful and happy

Gianluigi Buffon

ITALY

Hometown: Carrara

17

Buffon's age when he made his Serie A debut with Parma

Ht: 6' 3" • **Wt:** 175 • **DOB:** 1/28/78

Position: Goalkeeper

2009–2010 Salary: $8.25 million

International goals/International caps:
0 goals/100 caps

Personal homepage:
www.gianluigibuffon.com

Did you know?: Buffon is known for his affable, fun personality and his often humorous quotes to the media

As a kid: Gianluigi comes from an athletic family: his mom threw the discus, his dad was a weightlifter, and his uncle was a legendary Italian keeper.

Favorite food: Pasta alla carbonara

Hobbies: Watching soccer and solving puzzles

Favorite music: Dance and opera

Cited by many pundits as the greatest goalkeeper in the world, Gianluigi Buffon has high expectations to live up to every time he takes the field. The Juventus man continually exceeds expectations, making spectacular saves when his team needs him the most, earning him a reputation for clutch play that has only solidified his hold on the title of "best in the world."

In 2003, Buffon received the UEFA Most Valuable Player and Best Goalkeeper awards, and was named by Pelé as one of the top 125 greatest living footballers in March 2004. Despite stretches of tough play and a season in Serie B with Juventus, Buffon has managed to stay on top of the world of goalkeeping.

Buffon started out 2009–10 brilliantly, making a string of unbelievable saves in six straight games, renewing the calls from experts as the best keeper in the world.

Buffon's international career hit a skid during the Serie A betting scandal of 2006, but his team and fans stuck with him. He was a rock on the back line for Italy in the World Cup, backstopping the Italian's magical run to the title. He has remained the clear Number One for Italy, and as he nears his 100th cap, Buffon is more entrenched than perhaps any other keeper in the world.

"Gigi Buffon is in every way an original."

—Leo Turrini

"Van Persie continues to score what I call 'the goal of a lifetime.'"
—Arsenal manager Arsene Wegner

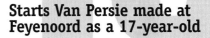

Robin Van Persie

NETHERLANDS

Hometown: Rotterdam

The recognizable face of Arsenal, Robin Van Persie is the kind of passionate, charismatic player that makes soccer fun to watch. Quickly approaching the 50-goal mark with Arsenal, Gunner fans have come to love Van Persie for his highlight-reel strikes.

The Netherlands have been a major beneficiary of Van Persie's scoring touch. Despite not being a regular starter for Arsenal, Van Persie was part of coach Marco van Basten's roster for the 2006 World Cup finals. He played in all four of the Netherlands' matches and scored his only goal in the group stage against Ivory Coast via a free kick as the Oranje were eliminated in the round of sixteen.

Van Persie scored a team-best four Euro 2008 qualifying goals and was deployed as a winger behind lone striker Ruud van Nistelrooy during the tournament after a formation switch. He finished Euro 2008 with two goals as the Netherlands finished atop their group but suffered a heartbreaking loss early in the knockout stages.

Van Persie played well during 2010 World Cup qualifiers, excelling all over the field in different situations, including assists off corners and header goals on corners, until an injury forced him to dial back his game a bit. He should be back in form by the start of the South Africa tournament, likely causing fits for opposing defenders.

Fast Stat:

15

Starts Van Persie made at Feyenoord as a 17-year-old

Ht: 6' • **Wt:** 155 • **DOB:** 8/6/83

Position: Striker

2009–2010 Salary: $6.8 million

International goals/International caps:
14 goals/40 caps

Personal homepage: none

Did you know?: Van Persie was voted Arsenal's player of the season for 2008–09 by the team's supporters.

As a kid: Van Persie was born with soccer in his blood, signing his first contract at age 14.

Favorite foods: Any Dutch food, pasta with meatballs

Hobbies: Spending time with his wife and kids

Favorite music: Anything to get pumped up and anything his kids like to listen to

Cristiano Ronaldo

PORTUGAL

Hometown: Madeira

Discovered by Manchester United manager Sir Alex Ferguson after a preseason exhibition match, Cristiano Ronaldo was one of Portugal's best-kept secrets throughout his youth years. Like most top-level professionals, Ronaldo became a solid player during his youth years, signing his first professional developmental deal at age 10. Quickly moving through the domestic league, Ronaldo found himself in the academy of the country's highest profile team, Sporting Lisbon.

Today he is one of the biggest superstars in the world of sport. The $131 million deal that brought him to Real Madrid was the biggest soccer news at the time, and his unveiling by the club was attended by more than 80,000 screaming fans.

Ronaldo has been a fixture on the Portuguese national team since 2003. He made the all-tournament team at Euro 2004 and hasn't slowed down since. Despite scoring only one goal at the 2006 World Cup, he carried his nation and was a constant thorn in opponent's sides during the team's run to the semifinals.

Known for his intensity and occasional theatrics and controversy on the field, Ronaldo is rarely doubted for his effort. Scoring multiple goals in several games during the 2006–2007 season, he was twice honored as the Premiership's Player of the Month during the season, a feat only three other players have accomplished.

With his performances at the club and international level, there is little doubt that Cristiano Ronaldo is one of the greatest players in the world. He is instantly recognizable and, love him or hate him, he brings large numbers of adoring fans to the sport.

Getty Images

"He's one of the most exciting young players I've ever seen."

—Manchester United manager Sir Alex Ferguson

Fast Stat:

17

Cristiano's age when Manchester United players convinced Manager Sir Alex Ferguson on a plane ride that they should sign him

Ht: 6' 1" • **Wt:** 180 • **DOB:** 2/5/85

Position: Wing

2009–2010 salary: $19.5 million

International goals/International caps: 22 goals/68 caps

Personal homepage: none

Did you know?: Cristiano scored two goals in his first senior game for Sporting Lisbon when he was just 16.

As a kid: A notable neighborhood street soccer player, Cristiano has been playing the game since age 3.

Favorite foods: Any seafood, but especially Portuguese codfish.

Hobbies: Watching movies, going on vacation, and the first day of soccer after a vacation

Favorite music: Ronalda, dance music, electronica, and techno

Getty Images

David Villa

SPAIN

Hometown: Tuilla

One of the finest strikers in the world, David Villa is one of the most in-demand players to ever hit the scene. Constantly linked with clubs all over Europe, the Valencia striker has been happy to ply his trade for his beloved club as well as be a dominating for the Spanish national team.

As a top player on one of the world's finest international squads, Villa is always under lots of pressure. Like a true champion, he always rises to meet the challenges and kick them in the teeth.

A successful season with Valencia saw him get called up as part of the 23-man squad to represent Spain at the 2006 FIFA World Cup. Spain's first match at the tournament and Villa's World Cup debut resulted in a 4–0 win against Ukraine in which the striker scored. He put in another goal against France in the round of 16, finishing tied with Fernando Torres as Spain's top scorer.

Villa carried his dominance into Euro 2008. He scored a hat trick in Spain's 4–1 win over Russia, making him the first player to do so at a UEFA European Championship since Patrick Kluivert in 2000 and only the seventh overall.

Scoring in Spain's first four qualifying matches for the World Cup, Villa again has proved himself to be the top player on perhaps the world's best team. Despite Spain's disappointing exit against the U.S. in the semifinals of the Confederations Cup, Villa has continued to pour goals in at a record pace, making him perhaps the face to watch in South Africa.

"I'd have David Villa over Kaká and Cristiano Ronaldo"

—Spain manager Vicente Del Bosque

Fast Stat:

13

Goals in 14 games for Villa in the 2008–09 international season

Ht: 5' 9" • **Wt:** 150 • **DOB:** 12/3/81

Position: Striker

2009–2010 Salary: Undisclosed

International goals/International caps: 33 goals/53 appearances

Personal homepage: www.davidvilla7.com

Did you know?: Every summer David hosts the "David Villa Camp," letting promising young players and down-on-their-luck kids play under the watchful eyes of top professionals.

As a kid: David suffered a tough leg break as a child that put his career in jeopardy. Luckily he made a full recovery.

Fun tidbit: David is one of just seven players to score a hat trick at the European Championships

Hobbies: Spending time with his family and watching movies

Favorite music: Spanish dance music and movie soundtracks

Fernando Torres

SPAIN

Hometown: Madrid

One of the top players in the world, Fernando Torres is a superstar on the rise, both in England and internationally. Discovered after a youth season in which he scored an impressive 55 goals from his striker position, Torres has been deadly in front of the net from his first kicks on. Since signing a youth deal with hometown club Atletico Madrid at the age of 11, Torres has become accustomed to success. Stints with Spain's Under-17 and World Cup teams have simply added to an impressive list of accolades that Torres has earned by the age of 25.

Torres is known not only for his pace, but for his technical skill. A fast mover with or without the ball, Torres is right-footed but is equally adept at striking or ball handling with either foot. One of the deadliest threats near the goal in European soccer (either in the air or on the ground), Torres will lay low before striking with deadly accuracy.

After five seasons with Atletico Madrid, it was a no-brainer that some of Europe's richest clubs would be after him. Eventually, Liverpool was the lucky squad, paying a club record transfer fee of more than $50 million to Atletico for Torres' services.

Paired with David Villa on Spain's national team, Torres makes the Spanish attack one of the world's most deadly, as seen at Euro 2008 when Spain won the championship. Torres was on fire in World Cup qualifying and other international play in 2009, including a hat trick in 14 minutes at the Confederations Cup against New Zealand. A man who never scores the same goal twice, Torres is poised for even greater success and is a player that fans should never take their eyes off of.

75

Goals Torres scored over five seasons in Spain, making him one of three men to accomplish the feat

Ht: 6' 1" • **Wt:** 170 • **DOB:** 3/20/84

Position: Striker

2009–2010 Salary: $9.56 million

International goals/International caps: 23 goals/71 caps

Personal homepage: www.fernando9torres.com

Did you know?: Liverpool paid a club record transfer fee to sign Torres

As a kid: Torres enjoyed two main hobbies as young child – playing soccer and throwing things out his parents' window. He played goalkeeper until he was nine.

Favorite foods: Any pasta.

Hobbies: Away from the field, Fernando enjoys spending time with his new wife and reading (mostly books about soccer)

Favorite music: Rock

Tim Cahill
AUSTRALIA
Hometown: Sydney

One of the most beloved players in the Premier League, Everton midfielder Tim Cahill is also respected on the international stage. The most visible face of a tough Australian "Socceroos" squad, Cahill is looking to take his team to new World Cup heights.

The midfielder made his debut for the Australian national team only in 2004, a result of his having played for Samoa at the U-17 level as a 14-year-old. A bit of an international enigma, in 2002 Cahill expressed a desire to play for the Republic of Ireland in the World Cup, even threatening a lawsuit to affirm Irish nationality.

Once he decided to represent Australia, his international career took off. The 2004 Oceania Player of the Year, Cahill played in the Olympics, his first major international tournament, that year. He is commonly referred to as "the super-sub" after two World Cup goals coming off the bench against Japan, and after saving Australia from an embarrassing defeat against Oman in their 2007 Asian Cup opener with a stoppage-time goal.

Cahill has struck many times in World Cup qualifying, quickly becoming the top choice Aussie goal scorer. His team will lean heavily on him in 2010, and since he's considered one of the best Australian players ever to don the uniform, he should be ready for the responsibility.

"Soccer is all about the journey."

Fast Stat:

20

Career header goals for Cahill, the most in Premier League history

Ht: 5' 10" • **Wt:** 152 • **DOB:** 12/6/79

Position: Attacking midfielder

2009–2010 Salary: $5 million

International goals/International caps:
19 goals/37 caps

Personal homepage: none

Did you know?: Cahill was the first Australian to ever score at the World Cup.

As a kid: Tim was encouraged to play sports, especially soccer, as a way to meet new friends.

Fun tidbit: Cahill is heavily involved in charity work, especially with UNICEF's children's charity.

Hobbies: Dancing, traveling

Favorite music: Folk rock and anything he can sing along to

Lionel Messi

ARGENTINA

Hometown: Rosario

Fast Stat:

17

Messi's age when he scored his first goal for Barcelona

Ht: 5' 6" • **Wt:** 147 • **DOB:** 6/24/87

Position: Midfield/Striker

2009–2010 Salary: $34 million

International goals/International caps: 13 goals/41 caps

Personal homepage: none

Did you know?: Lionel's middle name is Andres

As a kid: Lionel moved to Spain when he was just 13 to pursue his dream of playing pro soccer

Favorite food: Argentine barbeque

Hobbies: Lionel enjoys listening to traditional Argentine music and watching soccer on television

Favorite music: Samba, cumbi, and dance

A humble young man off of the soccer field, Lionel Messi is a dynamo on it. A spark plug that some say is worth more to his club than Ronaldinho ever was, Messi is poised to be the face of soccer in the 21st century. Already drawing comparisons to legendary Argentine Diego Maradona— some of those comments coming from Maradona himself—Messi has accomplished some amazing things even though he is only 22.

Messi has always played a big game. Signing with FC Barcelona at the age of 13, he made his debut with the side in 2003. At the age of 17, he became the youngest player ever to score for the club in league play.

His great passing and seemingly perfect on-field relationship with teammates even created competition over Messi on the international level. Offered a chance to jump ship and compete with the Spanish international team, Messi declined, keeping his loyalties with his native Argentina.

A big-match player, Messi was named to Argentina's squad for the 2006 World Cup. Although he did not appear in the team's first game and only came on as a late sub in the second, Messi was able to make a big impression. He assisted on a goal and scored another, making him the youngest goal scorer of the tournament. In all, the small Argentine superstar appeared in four games in his first World Cup, turning millions of heads around the world.

Though Argentina limped through qualifying for the 2010 World Cup, Messi led the team to the title in another recent major tournament: the 2008 Olympics. Seemingly coming through every time Argentina needed a big play, he assisted on the game-winning goal in the gold-medal match against Nigeria.

"I have seen the player who will inherit my place in Argentine football and his name is Messi."

—Argentina coach and soccer legend Diego Maradona

Kaka

BRAZIL

Hometown: Brasilia

A member of the latest generation of South American players to star in Europe, electrifying midfielder Kaka has enjoyed success after success in his career. Coming from a stable, middle-class family in Brazil, Kaka and his brother were gifted from a young age. After attending a local academy at age eight, Kaka signed his first pro contract at age 13. His rise was swift, and within seven years he had been named to Brazil's 2002 World Cup squad.

Kaka's time on that team was frustrating, however, as he observed more than he played. Only appearing in 18 minutes of action in a single game, he returned to his club with a new-found drive to be one of the world's best.

Returning to the World Cup in 2006, Kaka started the tournament off with a bang, scoring his team's only goal in their opening game win over Croatia. Unfortunately, the tournament went downhill from there—Kaka did not score again and Brazil was knocked out in the quarterfinals.

Possibly the most electrifying player currently lacing up the boots, Kaka was recently referred to by ESPN's Tommy Smyth as "the best player in the world today." The 2010 World Cup will be an opportunity for Kaka to seize the reins of a Brazil side in need of a leader to carry it deep into the knockout stages— and possibly to the championship.

A man of deep religious conviction, Kaka spends much of his offseason donating time to help the poor. Since 2006 he has been an ambassador for the United Nations' World Food Program, providing hope for people worldwide.

Fast Stat:

$115 million

Estimated fee that Real Madrid paid to buy Kaka from AC Milan

Ht: 6' 1" • **Wt:** 180 • **DOB:** 4/22/82

Position: Midfield

2009–2010 Salary: $15 million

International goals/International caps: 26 goals/73 caps

Personal homepage: none

Did you know?: Kaka was nearly paralyzed in a swimming accident when he was 18 but managed to make a full recovery.

As a kid: Kaka enjoyed playing soccer in the streets and on the beach, always teamed up with his brother.

Fun tidbit: Kaka's brother, Rodrigo, played with him at AC Milan and remains at the club.

Hobbies: Kaka enjoys spending time with his wife and family and playing beach soccer

Favorite music: Gospel

"Kaka has the potential to be the World Cup's most valuable player."

—Brazilian teammate Juninho

Robinho
BRAZIL
Hometown: Sao Vicente

"This lad will bring us a load of pleasure."
—Pele

One of the most-skilled players in soccer, Robinho has become known around the world. Thanks to his signature pedaling move and innate ability to control the game when he has the ball, Robinho has drawn praise from—and comparison to—Pele, the greatest to ever play the game. He is so skilled with the ball that he frequently pulls off what seems impossible for most players.

Carefully cultivated as a youth in Brazil, Robinho quickly showed himself to be among the top players in South America. He soon set his sights on Europe. Playing for one of the leading clubs in the world—Real Madrid—shined the spotlight on the young Brazilian, and he nearly melted under the pressure. Dribbling too much and embroiled in a contract dispute, Robinho took time to adjust to the European game. After three seasons in Madrid, he moved to Manchester City in the English Premiere League, leading the team in scoring in 2008–09. Rumors persist that he will someday return to Spain to play for Barcelona.

On the international stage, Robinho has played with the senior Brazilian soccer squad since 2003. Earning his first World Cup taste in 2006, Robinho played in every one of Brazil's games. He has captained Brazil once, and he played a major role in the team's 2009 Confederations Cup victory. The 2010 World Cup is coming perhaps at his peak, giving Robinho the chance to establish himself as one of the world's truly elite players.

Fast Stat:

73

Goals scored by Robinho as a nine-year-old

Ht: 5' 9" • **Wt:** 135 • **DOB:** 1/25/84

Position: Midfield/Striker

2009–2010 Salary: $13.7 million

International goals/International caps:
19 goals/71 caps

Personal homepage:
www.robinho.fobazo.com/en/static/1

Did you know?: Robinho joined the famous Brazilian national team at age 19

As a kid: Robinho was seemingly born with a ball and enjoyed playing beach soccer and futsal.

Favorite food: Brazilian barbeque

Hobbies: Beach soccer, practicing his footwork, playing practical jokes on teammates

Favorite music: Salsa

Michael Essien
GHANA
Hometown: Accra

One of the most versatile midfielders in the world, Michael Essien is comfortable anywhere on the pitch. Capable of shutting down opposing players or running free for a spectacular strike, the Chelsea man brings a big game every time he laces up his boots.

Even though he was one of the youngest players in the tournament, Essien took part in the 2001 FIFA World Youth Championship in Argentina. His exceptional performances captured the attention of many and he was tapped to be one of Africa's next big stars.

At the 2006 World Cup, Essien played a key role in helping Ghana become the only African team to reach the second round. Essien was suspended for the team's second round loss, feeding his fire to return to Cup finals in 2010 and improve his country's performance.

In the 2008 African Cup of Nations Essien turned in another brilliant performance, driving the team to the semifinals with his power-packed play, which earned him a nomination to the Team of the Tournament. Unfortunately, international competition took Essien away from soccer for much of the next season when he blew out his knee playing for Ghana in September 2008. He managed to recover and have a place in the country's qualifying matches, helping to carry the team to the top of its group and a spot in South Africa.

Fast Stat:

$40 million

Essien's transfer fee to Chelsea, at the time the largest sum ever been paid for an African player

Ht: 5' 10" • **Wt:** 170 • **DOB:** 12/3/1982

Position: Midfield/Defense

2009–2010 Salary: $7 million

International goals/International caps: 8 goals/45 caps

Personal homepage: www.michaelessiengh.com

Did you know?: Michael had a tryout with Manchester United in 2000, playing one game for their youth team.

As a kid: Michael was studious as a young man but loved soccer, dreaming of one day playing in Europe.

Fun tidbit: Essien is commonly referred to as "the Bison" for his hard-tackling, hard-nosed style on the pitch.

Hobbies: Playing video games, traveling, reading

Favorite music: European pop and rap, especially his own with Didier Drogba

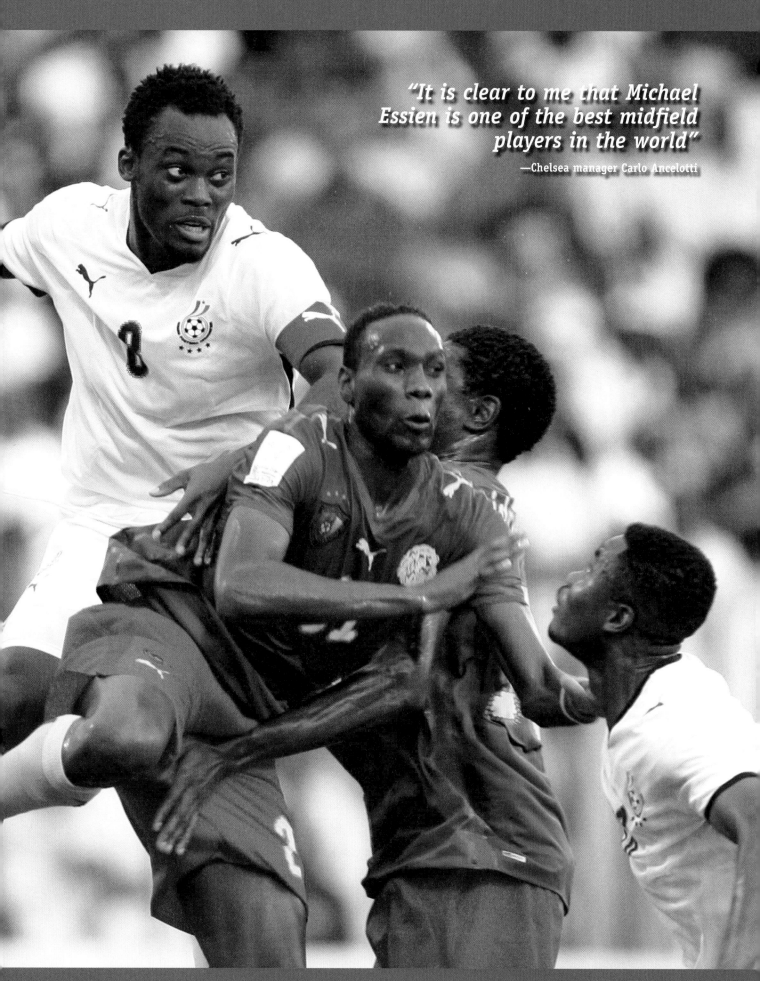

"It is clear to me that Michael Essien is one of the best midfield players in the world"
—Chelsea manager Carlo Ancelotti

"*Football's not an individual sport, you win and lose as a team.*"

Didier Drogba

IVORY COAST

Hometown: Abidjan

Getty Images

20

Premier League goals for Didier in 2007, the most in England

Ht: 6' 2" • **Wt:** 185 • **DOB:** 3/11/78

Position: Striker

2009–2010 Salary: $30 million

International goals/International caps: 41 goals/60 caps

Personal homepage: www.didierdrogba.com

Did you know?: Didier's two brothers are both professional soccer players.

As a kid: Didier spent three years living with relatives in France, but he grew homesick and eventually moved back home with his parents—though the family later settled in France permanently.

Favorite foods: Red meat, garlic, and traditional home cooking

Hobbies: Spending time with his three children

Favorite music: Rap and traditional African

When he's as healthy as he has been for the last two seasons, there may not be a more dangerous striker in the world than Didier Drogba. He's strong, speedy, and deadly accurate with both his feet and head. The Chelsea man started the 2009–2010 season hot in the FA Community Shield and he's finally showing the consistency that has sometimes undermined his considerable talents.

Drogba is an Ivory Coast (Côte d'Ivoire) international despite spending significant portions of his childhood in France. He's a vital part of the Ivorian squad, and he helped carry the country to its first World Cup appearance in 2006, with Drogba providing the bulk of the offense. He scored nine goals in eight qualifying games—statistically one of the best records in international soccer. In February 2005 he was voted runner-up to Samuel Eto'o in the African Footballer of the Year awards.

In February 2006, Drogba captained Ivory Coast to their second African Cup of Nations final, scoring the only goal in their semi-final match with Nigeria and putting away the deciding spot-kick in their record-tying 12–11 penalty shootout quarterfinal win over Cameroon.

In the 2008 African Cup of Nations, Ivory Coast made it to the semifinals, only to lose to perennial nemesis Egypt. As the team's top scorer, however, Drogba put on a good show. As he carries them forward to the 2010 global tournament, Ivory Coast can expect more top-notch performances from its best player. Defenders unlucky enough to face him in South Africa should have to much to fear.

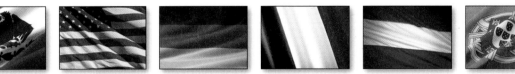

World Cup All-Time Results

Year	Host Country	Winner	Score
1930	Uruguay	Uruguay	Uruguay 4, Argentina 2
1934	Italy	Italy	Italy 2, Czechoslovakia 1
1938	France	Italy	Italy 4, Hungary 2
1942	not held	not held	not held
1946	not held	not held	not held
1950	Brazil	Uruguay	Uruguay 2, Brazil 1
1954	Switzerland	Germany	Germany 3, Hungary 2
1958	Sweden	Brazil	Brazil 5, Sweden 2
1962	Chile	Brazil	Brazil 3, Czechoslovakia 1
1966	England	England	England 4, Germany 2
1970	Mexico	Brazil	Brazil 4, Italy 1
1974	Germany	Germany	Germany 2, Netherlands 1
1978	Argentina	Argentina	Argentina 3, Netherlands 1
1982	Spain	Italy	Italy 3, Germany 1
1986	Mexico	Argentina	Argentina 3, Germany 2
1990	Italy	Germany	Germany 1, Argentina 0
1994	US	Brazil	Brazil 3, Italy 2
1998	France	France	France 3, Brazil 0
2002	Japan/South Korea	Brazil	Brazil 2, Germany 0
2006	Germany	Italy	Italy 1 (5-3), France 1